OYSTERING, OYSTERS, AND OTHER BIVALVES

OYSTERING, OYSTERS, AND OTHER BIVALVES

POEMS

WAYNE W. LYSOBEY

CONTENTS

SHUCKED

Shucked on shell on plate they lie
For lemon and some sauce they cry
Calling calling sensations bold
Let briny taste now quick unfold

WAYNE W. LYSOBEY

OYSTER BOY

There was a kid Jimmy they called oyster boy
Raking up oysters was his biggest joy
He was so happy to fill his red wagon
If he'd been a puppy his tail he'd be waggin'
Now he's grown up and called oyster Man
And he's dredging up oysters for raw bar and pan
But sometimes you might catch
A small smile on his face
When he remembers his red wagon oysterin' days

BEHOLD THE OYSTER

Behold the mighty oyster
So tender and so moister
Slid down raw never tires the jaw
While just lightly stewed
Are just slightly chewed

WAYNE W. LYSOBEY

OYSTER WORLD

The oyster was his world
The world was his oyster
He shucked and smiled
And smiled and shucked
He opened by the bushel
He opened by the truck
He shucked up a boatload
He called out for more
Finally tired
He shucked the last one
And that my dear friends
Is what he calls fun!

OYSTER SHUCKER

I got me an oyster knife
I thought I'd be a shucker
I tried it on the first one
It was a really stubborn trucker

I tried it on another
This one made me pucker
The shell it sliced my finger
That lousy bivalve mucker

I stuck one right in the hinge
And gave a mighty twist
The oyster did not budge
Now I was getting pissed

I started getting serious
I gave a satisfying curse
I put some muscle into it
Things went from bad to worse

The oyster knife it did slip
Jamming right into my wrist
I was dying for an oyster
Now I just might get my wish

THE OYSTER AWAITS

For common man and king
The oyster doth await
They lieth there on half shell
About to meet their fate

Be you pauper, be you prince
The feast is for the taking
Your station matters little now
When your taste buds do awaken

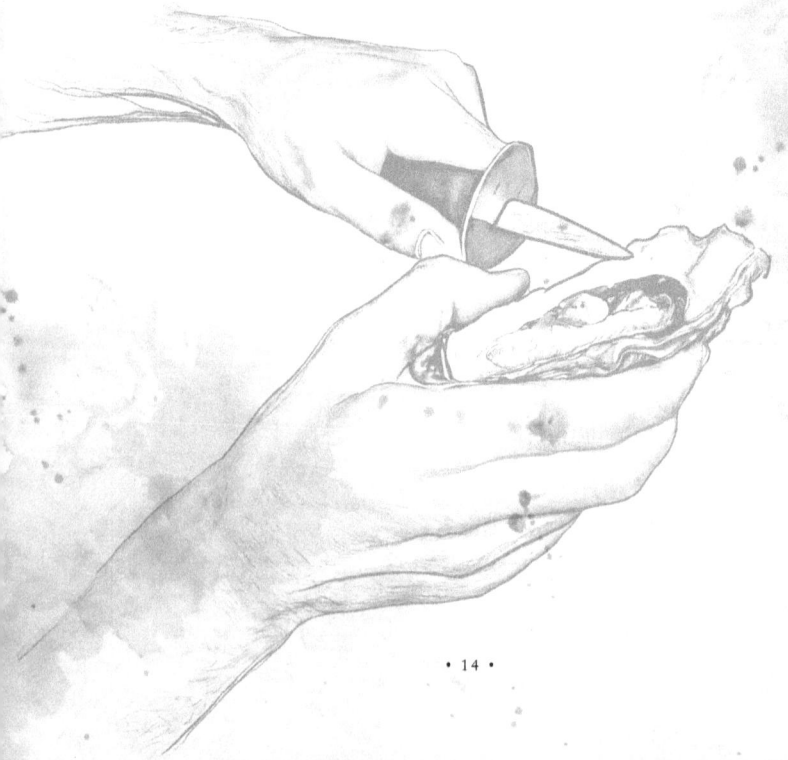

WAYNE W. LYSOBEY

WHITBECK

There once was a man named Whitbeck
He ate oysters by bushel and peck
Be they baked or they stewed
Or just lightly chewed
He'd say just a few more what the heck

OYSTER BILL

Oyster Bill ate oysters for snacks
He slurped one just right where he sat
He thought such a great pile
It may take quite a while
When he finished he felt a bit fat

WAYNE W. LYSOBEY

THE OYSTER EROTIC

Oh oyster so lovely
Laying naked in your shell
Awakening the senses so
You aphrodisiacal tease
Oh oyster oh oyster
What troubles have you done

PLATTER

Horseradish and ketchup
Made a little sauce
Some lime and some lemon
Sliced up for the cause

I did a little shuckin'
I put them on a platter
I did a little slurpin'
With just a little splatter

Oysters slid down raw
Really quite divine
Clams on the half hell
All washed down with wine

WAYNE W. LYSOBEY

HOW TO SHUCK AN OYSTER

Wiggle and worry that blade
Right into the hinge
Don't try to jam it
That's not the way to get in

Worry and wiggle
Till the knife's got a bite
Then give a firm twist
It should pop up just right

Now slide down that blade
The hard part is done
Cut the top of the muscle
It gets to be fun

Then swoop to the bottom
And try to cut clean
Try doing a dozen
And see what I mean

LIVE LONGER LOVE BETTER

Live longer love better
Tis wisdom quite old
So eat up your oysters
Live lively love bold

Just tilt back your head
Slide down a few raw
Tis with briny delight
You'll soon hold them in awe

Have some at midnight
And have some at lunch
Try some at supper
And have some at brunch

Get your omega three's
And your vitamins too
Slide down them oysters
That's so good for you

WAYNE W. LYSOBEY

ON THE HALF SHELL

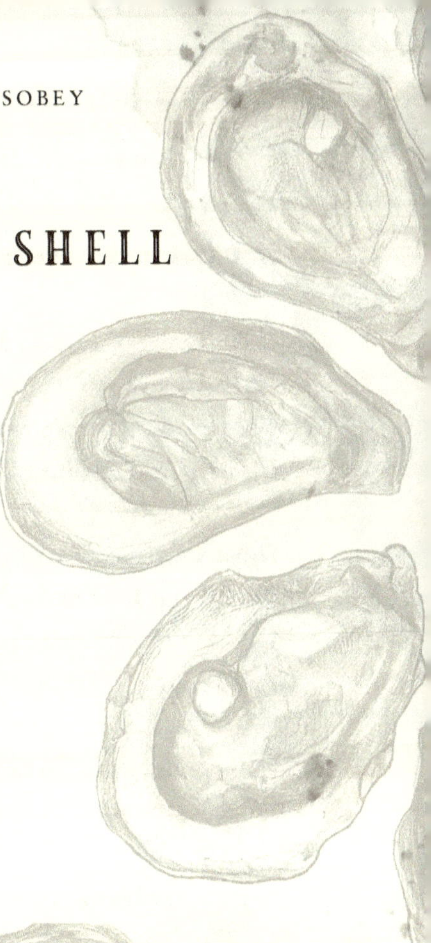

Oh stir the taste buds
With briny delight
Oysters on half shell
We be shucking tonight

Oh ready the lemon
And sauce of your favor
Littlenecks on half shell
With heavenly flavor

Oh transcendent table
And sumptuous repast
The taste of the sea
Right there in our grasp

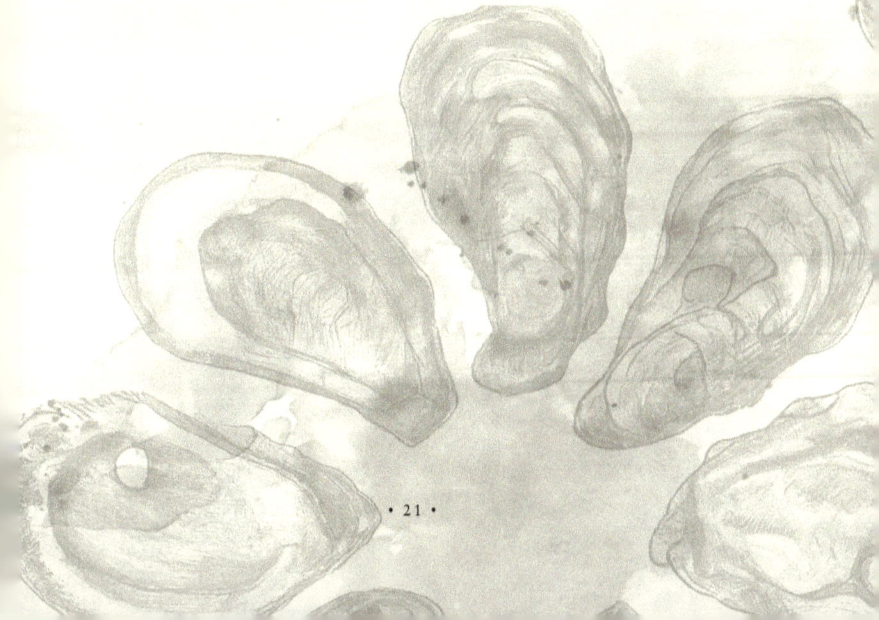

OYSTER DAYS

There were my days of dredgin' for oysters
Those bivalves so succulent tender and moister
Wonderful memories from my salty past
Though probably best that they didn't last

Those were the days of oyster romancin'
Out in your boat and set your dredge dancin'
Minds they were weak but backs they were strong
Tis likely a good thing those days are long gone

There in my shop the dredge hangs on the wall
On occasion I still feel the salt waters call
The salt and the shell the rocks and the mud
Just a bit of them oysters got into my blood

WAYNE W. LYSOBEY

A GOOD DAYS' HAUL

A good day of oystering
Is as good as any good day
The joy of a full dredge
And a salty breeze
Do calm the heart and soul
How welcome the sounds
Of oysters spilling onto the deck
The splash of the hungry dredge
The happy cries of gulls above
And how content the feeling
Of a good days' haul

A DOZEN WAYS

A dozen ways to oyster heaven
A dozen ways to bliss
See me here I'm waiting
Please put some on my dish

Will there be some on the half shell
Will there be a few stewed
They can be so good fried
Please bake some up too

With sauces with shallots
With some bacon and wine
With jalapeno lime butter
They taste quite divine

So don't keep me waiting
Start shucking them soon
For oysters have powers
That can make diners swoon

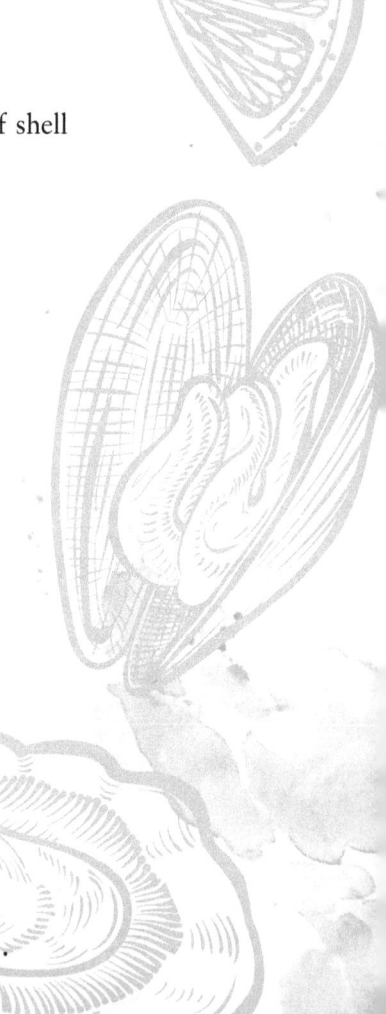

BIG EDDY

Big Eddy was a seed oyster man
Like Santa a right jolly old elf
He'd hoist his dredge onto his boat
Without even straining himself

Now that dredge was a widow maker
To use it not many were able
But Eddy would laugh while he dumped it
And covered his whole cullin' table

Then with a chuckle he'd toss it
Back for more oysters to catch
His hauls became stuff of legend
Which no other man could match

In them days we were all pretty tough
Slackers they would quickly fade
But none there was that matched the stuff
Of which good old Eddy was made

DUAL EXHAUST

There was the day of Acadama
Oh that sweet plum wine
The oyster bed was cleaned up
It was a celebration time

Now just why Eddy had that case
Oh that Acadama plum wine
Some thinks it fell off a truck
A rather fortuitous find

Eddy opened up one bottle
And another and another
A small group of oystermen
Became a band of brothers

So many bottles passed around
I found I had one in each hand
So I held both up to my lips
Now ain't life sweet and grand

Dual Exhaust I did exclaim
It became our drinking song
Wine and laughter it did flow
Now how can that be wrong

WAYNE W. LYSOBEY

OYSTERMEN I.

Oystermen are seedy characters
There is no doubt about that
And if you ever confront one
You might get into a spat

OYSTERMEN II.

Oystermen are set in their ways
They spend so much time in their beds
They muck about in their rubber boots
And their dredges need to be fed

OYSTERMEN III.

The cutting edge of oysters
Has sliced through many a glove
And the good sting of salt water
Does mix with oystermen blood

OYSTERMEN IV.

Whether it be the sweat of summer
Or the winter's bitter chill
The oyster boats go in an out
Till the culling tables are filled

WAYNE W. LYSOBEY

HALF SHELLS

Oh oysters on the half shell
I couldn't hardly wait
They brought them to my table
They put them on my plate

Oh oysters on the half shell
I was about to slurp you down
Was then I was distracted
Was then I turned around

Oh oysters on the half shell
I realized my greatest fear
I turned away for but a minute
And the oysters disappeared

OYSTER THIEF

There was a surreptitious slurper
An oyster gourmand of renown
Famous for stealing oysters
When you were turned around

Oysters off the half shell
Were stolen in a wink
Some thought this fiend four footed
At least that's what I think

A shaggy dog so friendly
At least that's what he seemed
Was spotted slurping oysters
And running from the scene

WAYNE W. LYSOBEY

OYSTERS

They spawned and then had quite a spat
Attachments they made where they sat
They filtered and fed
Laying in their own bed
Then dredged up when they'd gotten fat

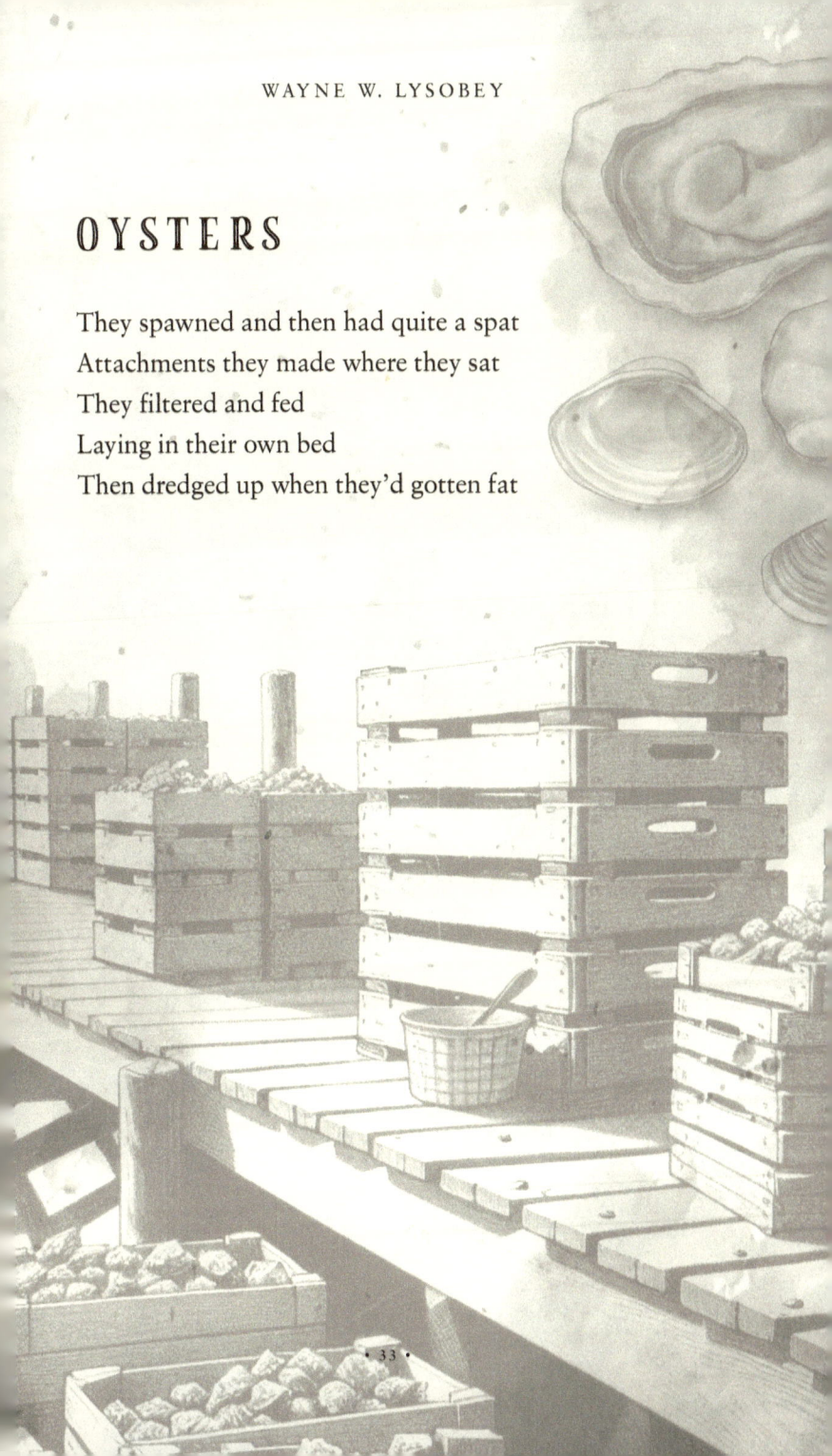

OYSTER FATE

Oh the injustice
Oh what a fate
Where are the oysters
To go on my plate

Oh the cruelty
Oh the crime
Where are the oysters
To have when I dine

Where is that salty
Taste of the sea
Please bring some
Please bring some
Some oysters to me

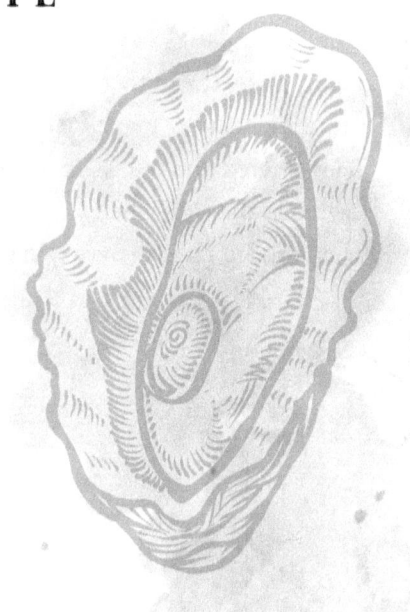

WAYNE W. LYSOBEY

BIVALVE REUNION

At the bivalve annual picnic
The Steamers they got really steamed
The Mussels tried to muscle in
The Scallops they got creamed

The Quahogs they did clam up
When the chowder did not last
The Littlenecks finally opened up
With cocktail sauce they got passed

The Cherries were off by themselves
Looked like they were getting stoned
An oyster crab got orphaned
And went looking for a home

The Razor Clams were finely honed
Some Mussels they did shave
They got into the beer tent
Where they were not well behaved

The Geoducks they came this year
They were philosophical and deep
Some Angel Clams did hover near
A pious bearing they did keep

The Oysters got a raw deal
When they sat down at the bar
A Walrus crashed the party
Saying best picnic by far

OYSTERS

Shuck 'em bake 'em
Put 'em on a plate
So many ways to have them
And all of them are great

WAYNE W. LYSOBEY

OYSTERS WERE SHUCKED

Oysters were shucked
Clams they were grilled
The weather was perfect
The people were thrilled

Smiles were rampant
Friends they were made
Thirst it was quenched
And appetites staid

The setting idyllic
An island oasis
The sun and the breeze
And hosts were most gracious

Good times they were had
By all that were there
Summer time memories
Long will be shared

OYSTERS OYSTERS

Oysters oysters
Plumper and moister
Squeeze of lemon
Bit of sauce
Slurp them slurp them
With no remorse
Eat them eat them
Briny delight
No need for
Second course
Tonight

OYSTERS I'M THINKING

Oysters I'm thinking
Oysters I'm craving
Without oysters soon
Mad I'll be raving

Oh give me some oysters
With Riesling well chilled
Forever with bliss
Then life will be filled

I'll have oysters well cooked
And a few slid down raw
Oysters oh oysters
I hold them in awe

Oysters oh oysters
My world you have shook
So sensuous raw
And so tasty cooked

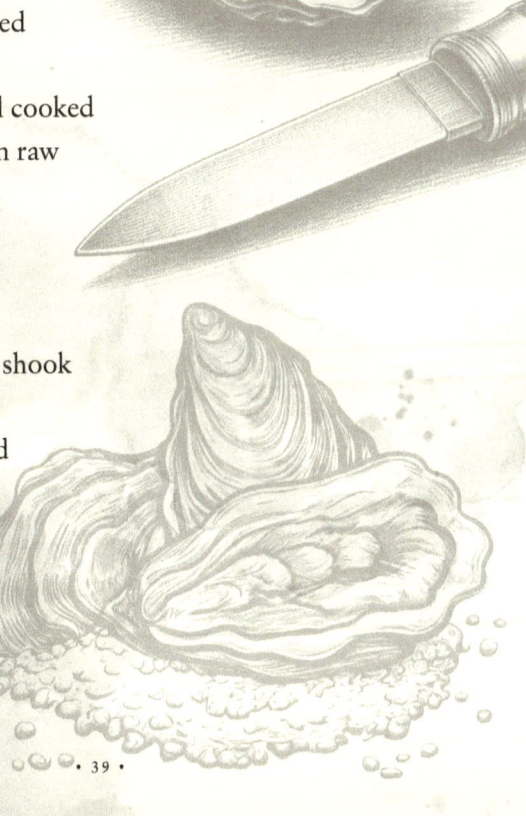

SARA L

Rotted timber
Worm eaten
And forgotten
Except by a few

In her day
Starfish moppin'
Oyster dredgin'
Oak ribbed proud

Sprite Island Ferry
Families and friends
Moonlight cruises

Nevermore

WAYNE W. LYSOBEY

OYSTER PLATTER

It was an oyster platter
Till the mussels muscled in
Some shrimps found a little spot
They lay there and they grinned
The lemon felt a bit squeezed
Clams clamored for attention
And did just what they pleased
Now the sauce was feeling saucy
And taste buds they did tease
The oysters they did give up grounds
And said let the feast begin
Then a walrus saw the platter
And he just dove right in

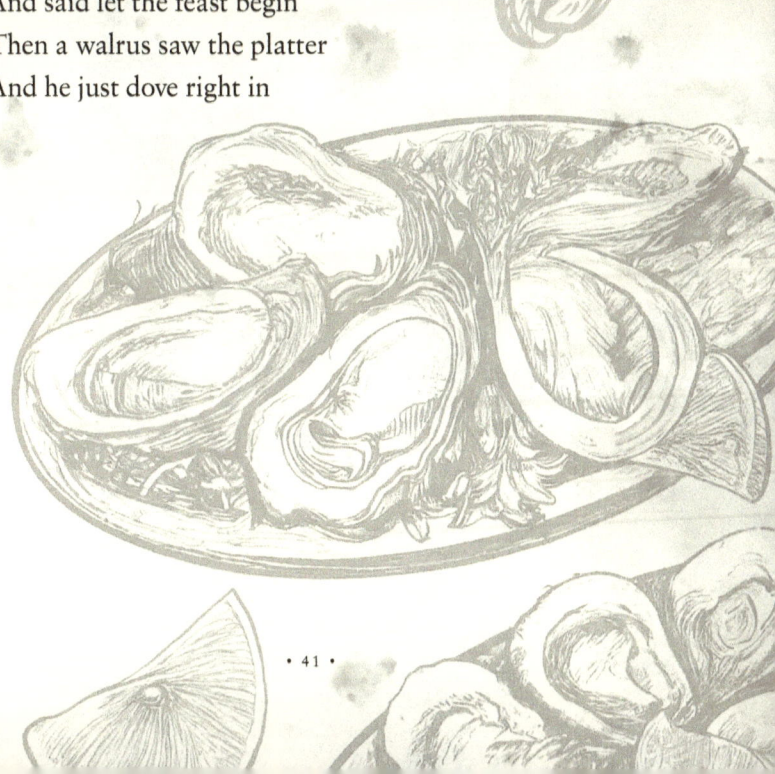

SCALLOPS

Scallops he shucked
Deft was his touch
The scallops they flew
The pile it grew
Then word got around
Dana's chowin' down
Though he did love to share
He had to beware
Or chances were thin
There'd be much left for him

WAYNE W. LYSOBEY

GEODUCK FARMER

Oh I want to be a geoduck farmer
And get right down in the muck
I might buy me a geoduck farm
I just hope in the mud I'm not stuck

They really do look a bit phallic
With that squirting and protruding neck
I'll say that they're completely orgasmic
And double the price what the heck

It might be my retirement business
I think that would be really grand
They are eaten sautéed or sashimi
I could open a geoduck stand!

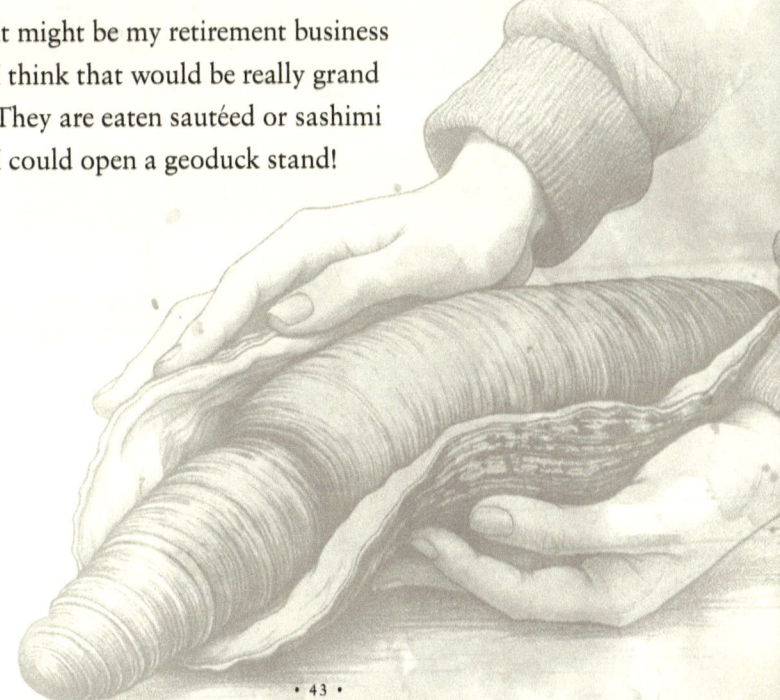

COPPS ISLAND OYSTERS

Round Copps Island they have the best oysters
They are succulent tender and moister
Bivalves there are best
Just give them the test
Your love life and health will be bolstered

THE PLATTER

Once again the platter was laid
And oh what a beautiful sight
Oysters nestled on half shell
An artfully laid out delight

Once again the senses were played
With lemon and sauce they do right
Not knave nor king I have to say
Will eat any better tonight

TEN OYSTERS

I had ten oysters the other night
Only six of them worked
Four just weren't quite right

I had ten oysters just last week
Only seven of them worked
Three were a bit weak

I had ten oysters a few weeks back
Only eight of them worked
But boy, they picked up the slack

I had ten oysters late last year
Only nine of them worked
It may have been the beer

I had ten oysters back in my youth
I didn't need 'em much then
To tell you the truth

OYSTER HAIKU

An oyster haiku
I have written just for you
How shellfish of me

OYSTER HAIKU 2

Oh sexy oyster
Laying naked in your shell
Lasciviously

ANOTHER OYSTER POEM

Put some oysters in your diet
Eat one raw or you can fry it

You can have some on a shell
You can have them stuffed as well

Serve them at home you'll be a winner
Or you can get them out at dinner

Oysters make a fancy brunch
Or eat some quick and call it lunch

So put those oysters in your diet
Then make sure your friends do try it

WAYNE W. LYSOBEY

OYSTERS OH OYSTERS

Oysters stewed oysters raw
Oysters oysters eat them all

Oysters grilled and on a bun
Eat them eat them just for fun

Oyster oyster aphrodisiac
Give them a try give them a crack

Have them with steak have them with wine
Have then have them all the time

Some for breakfast some for lunch
Slurp some raw then fry a bunch

Oysters oh oysters share with friends
Then have a party and do it again

A BOAT AND A DREDGE

All I need is a boat and a dredge
With a hardy crewman or two
And I'll be content chasing the oyster
We'll be catchin' more than a few

And when I'm gone let my spirit fly
Like a gull on that salty breeze
And let the waves then whisper
An oysterman's soul's now at ease

APPENDIX

A FEW RECIPES FROM THE AUTHOR

OYSTER WITH BEEF TENDERLOIN APPETIZER

Shucked Oysters, medium size. Copps Island or Blue Points Oysters are superb for this.

Beef tenderloin thin 1/8" slices, enough to match the oysters–2"-3" longest dimension, season/w salt and pepper.

Freshly made simple cilantro sauce—blend a few garlic cloves with a handful of cilantro and good olive oil, add pinch of salt. Add enough oil to make a thin paste use store bought pesto for second best option.

Ground pepper, salt, cayenne

Heat pan medium hot. Add some oil to coat. Add pat of butter. Add beef on one side of the pan, add oysters on the other. Flip beef and oysters. Do not overcook!

Remove tenderloin slices and top with oyster. Skewer with toothpick and top with dash of cayenne and bit of pesto. Do your best to dress them nicely, they are about to meet their fate! You can serve on top of half shells. Warm up the shells a little first!

Get that chilled glass with extra super good dry Riesling. Get Brooks from Willamette, damn it, if I don't buy the last bottle first!

Serve.

Try not to feel too decadent!

Live longer, love longer. Eat Oysters! Drink good wine!

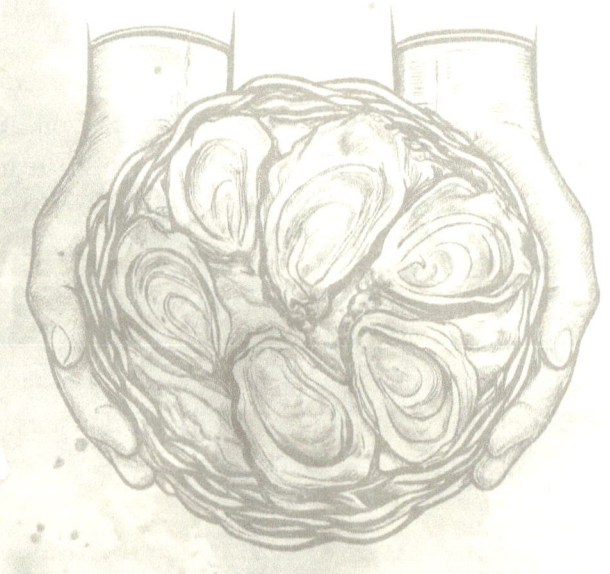

SAUTÉED OYSTERS ON TOAST POINTS

This is a favorite at home and about as simple as it gets.

Sautee 8 medium to large shucked oysters in a small pan with a pat of butter.

Add dash of cayenne to taste.

When they are curled on both sides they are done Don't overcook.

Serve immediately on toast points.

Best enjoyed in or near the kitchen!

Enjoy!

CLAMS WITH BROCCOLI RABE AND RICE

INGREDIENTS

2 lbs. little neck clams (or enough to mostly cover bottom of a 12" cast iron pan)

1 bunch broccoli rabe- chopped

1 1/2 cups long grain rice – uncooked

1 medium onion sliced

4-6 garlic cloves - smashed

Salt and Pepper

Dash of Cayenne optional

Olive Oil

PROCEDURE

Get clams ready ahead of time--rinse well, then cover with water. Sprinkle corn meal on top. Let sit one hour or up to overnight.

Preheat 12" cast iron pan or wok. Get rice cooking in your favorite rice pot or rice cooker.

Add some oil to pan. Throw in a smashed garlic clove. If or when it starts to sizzle, add rest of garlic and stir 1 minute. Add onion. Cook until it softens.

Throw broccoli rabe into pan. Turn up heat and cook 2-3 minutes. Remove broccoli rabe and onion to bowl, or throw on top of your rice, if your rice is ready.

Turn up heat, add rinsed clams and cover. In a few minutes, when clams start to open, add pepper to taste. Cover and cook until all clams are open.

Add rice and broccoli rabe. Taste. Add cayenne and/or salt if wanted. Stir together and cook for a minute or two. – If you do not have enough room, get out a good heavy bottom pot and add everything to that. Add some really good olive oil before serving.

Enjoy!

CLAMS WITH CHICKEN AND RICE

INGREDIENTS

2 lbs. little neck clams (or enough to mostly cover bottom of a 12" cast iron pan)

4 boneless skinless chicken thighs – cut stir fry size

2 cups long grain rice – uncooked

1 large onion sliced

6-10 garlic cloves - smashed

Chili Garlic sauce 1 teaspoon or to taste

Southwest Seasoning

Salt and Pepper

Canola or other cooking oil

PROCEDURE

Get clams ready ahead of time--rinse well, then cover with water. Sprinkle corn meal on top. Let sit one hour or up to overnight.

Preheat 12" cast iron pan. Get rice cooking in your favorite rice pot or rice cooker.

Add some oil to pan. Throw in a smashed garlic clove. If or when it starts to sizzle, add rest of garlic and stir 1 minute. Add onion. Cook until it softens.

Season chicken lightly with salt and liberally with Southwest Seasoning. Throw into pan. Turn up heat and stir until there is no pink left. Remove chicken and onion to bowl, or throw on top of your rice, if your rice is ready. Turn up heat, add rinsed clams and cover. In a few minutes, when clams start to open, add pepper to taste and chili garlic sauce. Cover and cook until all clams are open.

Add rice and chicken. Stir together and cook for a minute or two. If you do not have enough room, get out a good heavy bottom pot and add everything to that.

Did you chill the white wine? I recommend a nice dry Riesling.